ANTINO
AND LE

BY

J. L. HARRIS

CHAPTER TWO

LONDON • ENGLAND

ISBN 1 85307 124 2

DISTRIBUTORS

Bible, Book and Tract Depôt, 23 Santarosa Avenue, Ryde, NSW 2112, Australia
Bible House, Gateway Mall, 35 Tudor Street, Bridgetown, Barbados
Believers Bookshelf, 5205 Regional Road 81, Unit 3, Beamsville, ON, L0R 1B3, Canada
Bible Treasury Bookstore, 46 Queen Street, Dartmouth, Nova Scotia, B2Y 1G1, Canada
Bibles & Publications Chrétiennes, 30 rue Châteauvert, 26000 Valence, France
CSV, An der Schloßfabrik 30, 42499 Hückeswagen, Germany
Christian Truth Bookroom, Paddisonpet, Tenali 522 201, Andhra Pradesh, India
Words of Life Trust, 3 Chuim Village, Khar, Bombay, 400 052, India
Uit het Woord der Waarheid, Postbox 260, 7120AG Aalten, Netherlands
Bible and Book Depot, Box 25119, Christchurch 5, New Zealand
The Bookshelf, 263 St. Heliers Bay Road, Auckland 5, New Zealand
Echoes of Truth, P.O. Box 2637, Mushin, Lagos, Nigeria
Scripture Truth Publications, Box 6236, Surulere, Lagos, Nigeria
Kristen Literatur, Tjøsvoll øst, 4270 Åkrehamn, Norway
Beröa Verlag, Zellerstrasse 61, 8038 Zürich, Switzerland
Dépôt de Bibles et Traités Chrétiens, 4 rue du Nord, 1800 Vevey, Switzerland
Chapter Two Bookshop, 199 Plumstead Common Road, London, SE18 2UJ, UK
HoldFast Bible & Tract Depot, 100 Camden Road, Royal Tunbridge Wells, Kent, TN1 2QP, UK
Words of Truth, PO Box 147, Belfast, BT8 4TT, Northern Ireland, UK
Believers Bookshelf Inc., Box 261, Sunbury, PA 17801, USA

TYPESET BY CHAPTER TWO
Printed by How & Blackhall, Berwick upon Tweed

Antinomianism and Legalism

THE Law has ever furnished subject of disputation in the Church from the time of its earliest records. Some, by their strong assertions of Christians' liberty, have given occasion to others to turn the grace of God into licentiousness, because they have not perceived that the end of that liberty is service to God. "Being made free from sin and become servants to God, ye have your fruit unto holiness." (Romans 6:22) "As free and not using your liberty for a cloak of maliciousness, but as the servants of God." (1 Pet. 2:16) Christian liberty is in the Spirit, not in the flesh. Others have not only spoken, but acted as though we might sin, that grace might abound. They have asserted liberty for the flesh, and established that form of Antinomianism, which is apparently the counterpart of the doctrine of the Nicolaitans of old. "They speak great swelling words of vanity, they allure through the lusts of the flesh, through much wantonness, those that were clean escaped from them who live in error. While they promise them liberty, they themselves are the servants of corruption." (2 Peter 2:18-19) Such is the result of perverted and mutilated truth. And here the Legalist comes in and asserts the law to be the rule of Christian conduct, although they are delivered from it as the groundwork of justification. Such a statement carries with it great plausibility, but the principle is quite as erroneous as the one it would condemn; and it is remarkable how two such opposite principles alike result in a fearfully low exhibition of Christian character. "Some;" says the Apostle, "have turned aside unto vain jangling, desiring to be teachers of the Law, understanding neither what they say nor whereof they affirm." (1Timothy 1:6-7) Man to get rid of a difficulty of his own raising, has invented a theory which the Scriptures by no means warrant, for reconciling the grace of God in the salvation of His people, with the obligation they are under to serve Him. It is maintained that although the Law is not the ground of justification, it still remains the rule of Life. It is repealed in its condemning character, but unrepealed as a directory: - the ceremonial and civil part is abolished, but the moral remains obligatory. In every departure from Scripture there is danger; and I believe such a departure as the one above stated, to be attended with the most mischievous results. The Law is spoken of in Scripture as one thing. - "The Law was given by Moses" (John 1:17)

It is true the word Law is used in a less definite sense: but when the Law is used, it generally means the whole Mosaic economy, which was not partially but entirely superseded by that which was introduced by Christ. - "The Law was given by Moses, but grace and truth came by Jesus Christ." In no place in Scripture is that distinction found which is commonly insisted on between the moral and ceremonial law; - in this the Antinomian is right in principle. The Law was fulfilled and set aside by the work of Christ, in order to make way for the display of the wondrous grace of God. God in law is God imputing trespasses. It is true that such a distinction exactly suits our selfishness, which is to render unto God no more than He absolutely requires, which is just the principle of Law. It is obligation, it is duty, that which is rendered unwillingly, or which would not be rendered at all, were it not demanded. The mischief of such a statement I believe to be twofold. It tends to lead the children of God into bondage, and to lower their walk and conversation.

There is one sentence of the Apostle which exactly meets the difficulty. "Not without Law to God but under the Law to Christ." (1 Cor. 9:21) The article inserted in our translation confuses the sense - not lawless to God but under law to Christ. Here I believe the cases of the Antinomian and Legalist both to be met.

Whilst the Antinomian has clearly seen the putting away the Law, he has not seen the necessity of this in order to introduce a new relationship between God and man - even that of Father and Son. "God sent forth His Son made of a woman, made under the Law, to redeem them that were under the Law, that we might receive the adoption of sons. (Gal. 4:4,5) The law stood as a barrier to this, it was given to those who were servants, they were to do that which was commanded them, and then receive their wages; the principle was do and live. But the condition in which a Believer in Christ Jesus stands is very different: he is "no more a servant but a son; and if a son, then an heir of God through Christ." (Gal. 4:7) He is redeemed from the Law, he is dead to the Law, and the Law dead to him "by the body of Christ," (Rom. 7:4) it cannot attach to him in any way whatever. It is no longer the rule by which he walks, because being suitable for the relationship of master and servant, it is not suitable for the relationship of Father and son. The end proposed to those under the Law was obedience unto Life. "This do and thou shalt live." (Luke 10:28) But the result of that which in itself was good, and holy, and just, acting upon fallen man, was that it worked wrath and death. The Law could not give life, although it proposed it. But the Believer hath life, - "He that hath the son hath life;" (1 John 5:12) it is that from which he sets out, not that which he is pursuing. "Verily, verily I say unto you, he that heareth my words and believeth on Him that sent me, hath everlasting Life, and shall not come into judgement, but is passed from death unto life." (John 5:24) And as to the source of this Life, it is thus stated: "Blessed be God even the Father of our Lord Jesus Christ, who according to His abundant mercy, hath begotten us again unto a lively hope by the resurrection of Jesus Christ." (1 Pet. 1:3) "Of His own will begat He us." (James 1:18) The Believer is not therefore without Law to God, but the rule that subsisted between the Lord and the servant would not apply to his new relationship. And hence it is that not having been brought to know the Father, many a Christian, resting indeed on the all-sufficiency of the Atonement of Christ, does not stand fast in that liberty wherewith Christ has made him free. - "For ye are all the children of God by faith in Jesus Christ." (Gal. 3:26) And not rejoicing in the liberty of Sonship, they see not their calling to be to walk as "obedient children, not fashioning yourselves according to the former lusts in your ignorance, but as He which hath called them is Holy, so be ye holy in all manner of conversation." (1 Pet. 1:14-15)

They still look to the Law as their rule, and receive "the spirit of bondage again to fear", (Rom. 8:15) questioning as to the extent of the obedience required, instead of returning the answer of a willing heart unto a loving Father. The Law deals in formal enactments, but the Spirit, which is liberty, more in the application of some great and acknowledged principles. What Law could accurately define the measure and quality of the obedience of a child to a parent? It would be shown in an hundred ways which the loving heart would be quick-sighted in discovering, and none but the father's eye could detect. And is not this precisely the character of a Christian's obedience to his God? His liberty makes him not lawless to God, but his obedience is much carried out where no human eye can behold him. He prays, he fasts, he gives alms, in the presence of his "Father which seeth in secret." (Matt. 6:4) It is indeed blessed liberty into which we are called as children of God, but it is a high and holy responsibility. "Be ye therefore followers (imitators) of God as dear children and walk in love." (Eph. 5:1-2) The perfectness of the Father's love is the only standard proposed to the children. - "Be ye therefore perfect even as your Father which is in heaven is perfect." (Mat. 5:47) Just in proportion as the relationship is raised in dignity from that of a servant to that of a son, so is the standard of obedience raised also.

The Law might tend to tutor the flesh, but the Spirit alone could serve God. "If ye be led of the Spirit ye are not under the Law," (Gal. 5:18) and this applies to the Law as a rule of Life; for the question in this passage is not concerning justification, but Christian conduct. "This I say then, Walk in the Spirit and ye shall not fulfil the lust of the flesh." (Gal. 5:16) In Jesus we have One made under the Law, meeting every one of God's requirements, even fulfilling all righteousness; in Him also we have One led by the Spirit into the wilderness into conflict with Satan to show His perfect dependence as a Son. His obedience was beyond Law righteousness, for He became "obedient unto death, even the death of the Cross," (Phil. 2:8) "that the world might know that I love the Father, and that as the Father gave me commandment so I do." (John 14:31) He had right and title to have entered into life, because He had kept the commandments. But that life He laid down, "He had power to lay it down, and power to take it again;" (John 10:18) and His perfectness of obedience in this respect was so well pleasing to the Father- "Therefore doth my Father love me because I lay down my life." (John 10:17)

He, as the servant, met every requirement of the Law; but as the Son, carried His obedience on unto the entire surrender of His own will, to the will of Him who sent Him. And this sure standard does Jesus hold up to His followers; If, says He, speaking to the young man of great possessions (who evidently connected eternal life with earthly enjoyment), "If thou wilt enter into life, keep the commandments;" but "if thou wilt be perfect, go and sell that thou hast, and give to the poor, and thou shalt have treasure in heaven; and come follow me." (Matt. 19:17 & 21) It was His own entire self-renunciation which Jesus proposed as the standard of perfectness; not the servant under the Law, but "the Son learning obedience through the things that He suffered." (Heb. 5:8) surely then, freedom from the yoke of bondage, is not that we may be without Law to God, but that we may be obedient children. And the knowledge of the Father, whilst it is our most blessed and perfect security in the confidence of His ever watchful care and love, is at the same time His security against any abuse of that liberty into which we are called by His grace. It was the great object of Jesus to manifest the name of God, even the blessed name of Father, to those whom the Father had given Him out of the world, in order that by them that name might be hallowed. It is to the Father, as the Holy Father, and righteous Father, whom the world knew not, that He commends His disciples on leaving them, upon the ground that they knew Him as such, and therefore would reconcile that seeming paradox to the world, how at the same time a believer is living in the most perfect sense of security, and aiming to walk in perfect obedience. It is the righteous Father. There is no difficulty in this to one "led of the Spirit", (Gal. 5:18) yet I believe there always must be an insurmountable difficulty in putting theoretically before the minds of men Liberty and Obedience, so necessarily do they suppose the one to exclude the other.

But the consideration of the remainder of the Apostle's statement, as to a Christian being "under Law to Christ," (1 Cor. 9:21) will most plainly prove that he is in no sense whatever under the Law. "The Law is not made for a righteous Man, but for the lawless and disobedient, for the ungodly and for sinners, for unholy and profane." (1 Tim. 1:9) It may be used lawfully as the expression of God's mind with respect to a variety of actions; it may be used lawfully too as exhibiting any great principle of the divine conduct; as such the Apostle uses it, when insisting on children obeying their parents in the Lord, where he shows that there was in the Law an express promise to obedient children. So again he uses it lawfully when he presents it as the general expression of the divine mind, that labour of any kind is entitled to support. "Say I these things as a man? Or saith not the Law the same also? For it is written in the law of Moses, thou shalt not muzzle the mouth of the ox that treadeth out the corn." (1 Cor. 9:8,9) If we use it not thus, we deprive ourselves of the benefit of God's own expressed mind on a great variety of subjects[1] and therefore of that wisdom which cometh from above. But fully allowing all this, I would assert that the believer who proposed to himself the Law for his rule would constantly be walking disorderly as a disciple of Christ. It was given by Moses for a specific purpose, and especially in reference to earthly blessing. It met therefore, as far as it possibly could, man's weakness, as we find in the case of divorce. (Matt. 19:7,8) "It made nothing perfect" (Heb. 7:19) "Grace and truth came by Jesus Christ." (John 1:17) And we are under Law to Christ, not to Moses. This must appear immediately to any one marking the authority that the Lord Jesus Christ assumes to Himself in the sermon on the Mount. "It was said by them of old,.. but I say unto you,.. whosoever heareth these saying of mine." (Matt. 5:21 & 7:24) Christ being Mediator of the New Covenant "established upon better promises," (Heb. 8:6) the Rule of conduct must necessarily differ, even as the dispensation under which we are, essentially differs from the former. God in that, was dealing with man on the ground of righteousness; but with us, in grace. The blessing to which we are called, is heavenly; and the rule by which we are guided is the Rule of heaven. All the difficulties in walking by it, arise from the circumstances in which we are placed. To do God's will in heaven, where all is in accordance with that will, must be the highest

1. It is doubtless yet to be exhibited that God's own arrangements for securing earthly blessing are alone calculated for that end. But such arrangements cannot apply to the present dispensation.

blessedness to which a moral creature of any capacity can attain. "Bless the Lord, ye His angels that excel in strength, that do His commandments, hearkening unto the voice of His word. Bless ye the Lord all ye His hosts, ye ministers of His that do His pleasure." (Psalm 103:20,21) But to do God's will on earth, where all is disorder, is the great trial. There was One who did it perfectly, "Lo I come to do thy will O God." (Heb. 10:7) It was His alone to say, "Father I have glorified thee on the earth;" (John 17:4) and He who had done this was fully qualified to give us a directory, as well as to leave us "an example that ye should follow His steps." (1 Pet. 2:21)

But obedience to Law and protection from the Lawgiver are reciprocal. It is always supposed that the Legislator has power to protect those who own his authority, as well as punish those who do not. It is on the principle of ability to protect, that our Lord Jesus claims our unreserved obedience, "All power is given unto me in heaven and in earth, go ye therefore and teach all nations, baptizing them in the name of the Father, and of the Son, and of the Holy Ghost; teaching them to observe all things whatsoever I have commanded you; and lo I am with you always, even unto the end of the world." (Matt. 28:18-20) Now here the claim of our obedience is, that He has all power in heaven and in earth and is therefore fully able to keep those who acknowledge Him in His ways. It is therefore that the test of discipleship is the confession of His name as Lord, as well as Saviour. It is after He has given His disciples such directions, the following out of which would inevitably throw them against the whole course of this world, that He adds, "And why call ye me Lord, Lord, and do not the things which I say?" (Luke 6:46) And again, "Not every one that saith unto me Lord, Lord, shall enter into the kingdom of heaven, but he that doeth the will of my Father which is in heaven. Many will say unto me in that day, Lord, have we not prophesied in thy name...; and then will I profess unto them I never knew you, depart from me ye that work iniquity. (Matt. 7:21-23). He will not own that as confession unto Him, which does not show itself in subjection unto His word as authoritative. The whole of His directions for the conduct of His disciples assume the principle that they are heavenly men. He who, whilst on earth, was the son of Man in heaven, was the only One who ever passed through this world untainted by its evil; He overcame the world, and showed that implicit subjection to the word of God was the only safeguard against evil, - that God was the only wise God, whose wisdom could guide through the intricate maze of evil in which the world was and is. "Concerning the works of men, by the word of thy lips I have kept me from the paths of the destroyer." (Psalm 17:4) He met all evil in meekness and lowliness; but the Father was with Him. And that which He has given us is that wisdom which is from above, which is "pure, then peaceable, and gentle, and easy to be entreated, ... without partiality, and without hypocrisy." It is in everything the reverse of what man calls wisdom, because it overcomes by enduring, and not by avoiding or resisting. This wisdom is "hid ... from the wise and prudent" (Matt. 11:25) and given unto babes, as those whose place in this world is helplessness and exposure to danger. But here comes in the blessed understanding of power to protect in following out His commandments, which necessarily leads to suffering from the world. Here is the great need of recognizing the standing of a Christian, under law to Christ and not to Moses. It is to fidelity to Him in this that the Lord especially looks. The obedience of a Christian is the obedience of faith, the obedience of Law the obedience of sense. In the latter case to the Jew, as under the Law, the result of obedience was immediately manifested in blessing. Not so now (outwardly at least); but our calling is to patient continuance in well doing, "for in due season we shall reap if we faint not." (Gal. 6:9) We are called to sit down and count our cost, if we are content to follow Jesus out of the world; for assuredly His precepts do set a man entirely against it. And what, unless the assurance of competent protection in walking in His ways, from Him who could say, "All power is given unto me" (Matt. 28:20) can for a moment keep us in the narrow way that leadeth unto eternal life? What but the assurance of sufficiency of strength, from Him who says "Lo I am with you always, even unto the end of the world," could induce felt weakness to set itself in array against the enemies it has to contend with? "Who is sufficient for these things," (2 Cor. 2:16) can only be answered by "I can do all things through Christ strengthening me." (Phil. 4:13) It is most needful ever to associate in our thoughts the distinct character of the commandments of the Lord Jesus as leading to suffering in the world, with His power to keep and protect those who are walking in His ways. This is to walk by faith and not by sight. This is the happy deliverance from that perplexity which must ever meet one who knows no power above the will of this world; and who is therefore always calculating on results which may only disappoint him, or balancing evils to choose between them. The Christian, in proportion to his faith, is delivered from these; he has to expect from the world nothing but evil: "sufficient to the day is the evil thereof." (Matt. 6:34) And as to good, he knows that to be only the good, and perfect, and acceptable will of God. In taking that for his guide it may lead into humiliation and suffering, but the end is deliverance from evil. The prayer of Jesus for His disciples was not that they should be taken out of the world, but be kept from the evil - that they should occupy His standing and place in it. “The disciple is not above his Master, but every one that is perfect shall be as his Master” (Luke 6:40). And how is this to be but by keeping all things that He has commanded us. “We are not under the law but under grace.” (Rom. 6:14) And that which is required of those under the Law. We may notice this in a few striking instances. Under the Law, divorce was permitted on many accounts, under Christ, only in a case of fornication on either side. Under the Law, Polygamy was tolerated; but under Christ, in whom was shown the antitype of marriage, it is not permitted. Christ is one, and His Church is one, - so in the beginning, God, to show His plan, made them a male and a female. Under Moses a man was entitled to assert his right, and to receive compensation for injury; not so under Christ - “I say unto you resist not evil.” (Matt. 5:39) “Avenge not yourselves.” (Rom. 12:9) “Rather suffer wrong.” (1 Cor. 6:7) “Forgive till seventy times seven.” (Matt. 18:19) Under the Law it was permitted to amass treasures as the proof of God’s blessing; but Christ says, “Lay not up for yourselves treasures on the earth.” (Matt. 6:19) This might be followed out into lengthened detail, but enough has been said to show that to be under law to Christ, is to be under heavenly rule in the midst of evil; and therefore necessarily produces that wonderful anomaly in the present state which faith alone can clear up - righteousness suffering, and wickedness flourishing. "The earth is given into the hand of the wicked, he covereth the faces of the judges thereof: if not, where and who is he?" (Job 9:24)

In the present day when allegiance to Christ as their Lawgiver, has been so lamentably forgotten by the Lord's own people, when their fear towards Him in this character has been taught by the doctrines of men, it is only known to those who are seeking in simplicity to serve Him, how difficult is the obedience of faith. So intimately have the two directories of Law and Grace been accustomed to be blended, that many a Believer is found thinking, and speaking and acting unconsciously as a Jew. Men have gone on unconsciously confounding things that differ, so that the simplest commandment of the Lord or His Apostles, is often met by setting the conduct of a Patriarch, or the language of the Law against it. Hence we must needs discriminate between that which is Scriptural, and that which is Christian. For instance, war is scriptural: Jehovah Himself went forth as the Captain of Israel's host: but says Christ, "They that take the sword, shall perish with the sword." (Matt. 26:52) Vengeance is scriptural: the avenger of blood might pursue the murderer; but says the Spirit by the Apostle, "Avenge not yourselves." (Rom. 12:9)

But not only in these great things, but in things of minor importance (and fidelity to the Lord is therein much shown), shall we find occasion of confessing to Him as our Lord. Only let it ever be borne in mind, that it is because we are called to liberty, even the liberty of Sons, because we are already made of the household of God, and have our mansions prepared in it, that the Lord Jesus as Head over that house, claims our allegiance to Him. It is because we belong to heaven that He exercises this authority over us, in order that we may walk worthy of our high and holy calling. It is because we are Son, and if Sons then Heirs, Heirs of God and joint Heirs with Christ, that the Son who has made us free, shows us how to use that freedom in service to the Father. The Master of the house is absent for a while, but behold he cometh, and "that servant that knew his Lord's will, and prepared not himself, neither did according to His will, shall be beaten with many stripes." (Luke 12:47) Here it is that reasonings come in, and here the Spirit of God comes to bear, casting them down and bringing every thought into captivity to the obedience of Christ. I believe obedience to Christ to be now of great difficulty, from lack of that Spirit in power to make use of quick understanding in the fear of the Lord, from our having been so habituated to act on results instead of Faith. The Lord does not show His people how they are to be kept, or what will be the consequence of their acting in obedience to Him. But He will *with* the trial, make a way for them to escape. And if any man will do His will, he shall know the blessedness afterwards. It is astonishing how little any are able, from the habit of looking at consequences, to judge righteous judgement. The Apostle prays for the Philippians, that their love might abound more and more in knowledge, and in all judgement (spiritual apprehension): that they might approve things that were excellent, and be sincere and without offence till the day of Christ. From the habit of not comparing things with the Truth, but with one another, very few are capable of estimating the principles on which they are acting. A very great principle may be involved in a very trivial action; and here the craft of Satan works, as we may see in the temptation of our Lord; his object is to undermine a principle, and then the people of God are tossed to and fro, and hindered in their service to the Lord. And what will be security against him whose coming is "after the working of Satan, with … all deceivableness of unrighteousness," (2 Thess. 2:9-10) but simple dependence on the blood of the Lamb, and on the Word He hath given us for our guidance? The time calls for decision. He that is not with Christ, is against Him. Fidelity to Christ is protest against evil, for what concord hath Christ with Belial? The path may be difficult, because so many things good and useful in themselves, are mingled with that which is evil; but the Comforter, "...the Spirit of truth," will guide into all truth. Satan's object is to accredit the evil, by mingling it with good. Ours must be to discriminate between them, "to prove all things and hold fast that which is good." (1 Thess. 5:21) As under law to Christ, our calling is, not to be "ashamed of the testimony of our Lord," ... "but be partakers of the afflictions of the Gospel, according to the power of God." (2 Tim. 1:8) There is, now, as in the close of the Apostle's career, more trial from the worldliness of disciples, than from the persecution of the world. May then the last charge of the Apostle to his beloved Timothy, be written on our hearts, "Thou therefore endure hardness as a good soldier of Jesus Christ; no man that warreth entangleth himself with the affairs of this life, that he may please him who hath called him to be a soldier." (2 Tim. 2:3-4) "So run that ye may obtain." (1 Cor. 9:24)

Other titles in the Booklet series

- **The Eternal Son of the Father**. by W. R. Dronsfield
  2nd Edition 1 85307 018 1
- **Unity and Authority**. by W. R. Dronsfield
  1 85307 030 0
- **Kings and Priests, Ritualism.** by William Kelly
  1 85307 107 2
- **Marriages are Made in Heaven**. by Allan Retallick
  0 947588 03 5
- **The Way of Faith in an Evil Time**. by H. H. Snell
  1 85307 099 8

other titles in preparation

available direct from the publishers:

Chapter Two, 13 Plum Lane, London SE18 3AF UK

or through any good Christian book shop